Original title:
Moonlight in the Meadow

Copyright © 2025 Creative Arts Management OÜ
All rights reserved.

Author: Finn Donovan
ISBN HARDBACK: 978-1-80567-240-1
ISBN PAPERBACK: 978-1-80567-539-6

The Night's Caress over Still Blades

The grass lies flat, a sleepy cat,
Dreams are stitched in twinkling spat.
An owl hoots jokes, all quite absurd,
While crickets join the nightly herd.

The fireflies blink, a crazy show,
They dance around like they don't know.
One lands on my nose, ticklish and bright,
I sneeze and scare the bugs in flight!

Dappled Dreams Beneath the Starlit Sky

Stars are peekaboo in playful guise,
While cows compete in moos and sighs.
A raccoon steals snacks, quite the thief,
It winks at me, what a funny brief!

The breeze makes whispers that tease my ear,
It tells me jokes, some kind of cheer.
A frog croaks loud, a silly dispute,
With lightning bugs that just won't scoot!

Ethereal Beauty of Night's Tapestry

The blanket shines with soft, bright dots,
While dancing moths confuse the pots.
A gang of geese start a bizarre choir,
Honking along like they're on fire!

Each blade of grass is a giggling friend,
They sway and nod, on laughter depend.
The breeze trips over a sleepy hare,
Who jumps and stares, a baffled glare!

A Dance with the Whispering Breeze

The playful wind takes hold of my hat,
Spins it around, oh look at that!
A squirrel looks on, rolling in mirth,
As I chase my cap, for what it's worth!

A group of stars starts to chuckle and wink,
As shadows gather making me think.
Why do the trees sway and shake with glee?
Is it just me, or are they teasing me?

Whispers of Twilight Serenade

When owls begin their silly dance,
A rabbit leaps in a comical prance.
The crickets chirp their offbeat tune,
While fireflies do their daytime swoon.

Grasshoppers hop like they own the place,
Spinning stories with a vibrant grace.
Each flicker of light brings giggles galore,
As stars wink down, asking for more.

Luminous Dreams on Gentle Grass

A hedgehog dons a tiny sombrero,
While dancing with a bold little sparrow.
The winds giggle, swirling all around,
As flowers chuckle with a rustling sound.

Silly shadows play tag on the hill,
Each flicker of night brings another thrill.
With nibbled snacks and laughter in air,
Creatures gather, a joyful affair.

Silvery Shadows Beneath the Stars

Beneath the twinkling lights so clear,
A raccoon's joke brings a chipmunk cheer.
The hedges sway with a juicy tale,
Of lost socks in the fiery gale.

A turtle makes a daring bet,
To outrun a leaf on a strange fret.
While sleepy daisies clink their cups,
As whimsical laughter fills the ups.

Night's Embrace upon the Fields

In the stillness where shadows piqué,
A goat is singing a wobbly spree.
With each blaring note, the night takes flight,
As stars giggle and boost the delight.

Squirrels toss acorns, like popcorn in air,
Creating a ruckus that's far from rare.
The breeze carries secrets from friends afar,
Underneath the watchful eye of a star.

Delight in the Stillness of Darkness

When shadows dance and play,
The critters come out to sway.
A squirrel with flair takes the lead,
As fireflies twinkle with speed.

The owl lets out a hoot so wise,
While rabbits hop in a soft disguise.
They laugh at the stars, so bold and bright,
In a revelry of pure delight.

Mysterious Glow in the Field of Dreams

In the hush of night, a glow spills wide,
A glowworm's dance, no need to hide.
The grass sings with giggles, soft and low,
As crickets join in, buzzing to and fro.

A cow stumbles upon the scene,
With a moo that erupts—a comical queen!
She twirls in joy, causing a stir,
While frogs croak their tunes, what a blur!

Enigmatic Light on Gentle Slopes

The hills are alive with a flickering light,
As rabbits hold a dance-off, oh what a sight!
With cartwheels and flips, they hop with glee,
While owls in tuxedos offer VIP.

A hedgehog spins like a tiny top,
While a wise old cat just smiles and stops.
"Don't mind the chaos," he says with a purr,
"It's just nature's party, let's all concur!"

Whispers of the Silver Glow

Soft whispers float through the cool night air,
As mice hold a meeting, discussing with flair.
"What should we wear?" one squeaks with a grin,
"Let's dress as fancy as we can, my kin!"

The hedgehogs chime in, adorned in spines,
While the owls critique, sipping on wines.
A bashful badger drops in by chance,
To join the fun, and join the dance!

Emotions Stirred Beneath the Celestial Glow

In the pasture so bright, the cows start to prance,
Beneath a great shimmer, they join in a dance.
A firefly's glow causes quite the confusion,
As critters all wiggle in silly exclusion.

A rabbit with goggles rides high on a goat,
While singing a tune, 'I can totally float!'
Goats roll their eyes, they know it's a joke,
But the laughter erupts, and all of them cloak.

The owls are hooting with mischievous glee,
As squirrels start plotting a giggling spree.
The stars twinkle bright as if laughing, you see,
As raccoons share secrets with just a loud squeak.

With shadows that dance 'neath the shimmering dome,
All creatures conspire to make this their home.
In fits of delight, they frolic and play,
Under the soft glow, they all shout hooray!

Shimmering Traces Amongst the Flora

In the grass, a frog did sing,
Wearing leaves as a fancy ring.
Fireflies danced in silly flight,
Turning the night into a slight fright.

Bees wore hats, how absurd and bright,
Buzzing tales of their grand night.
A rabbit juggled carrots with glee,
Wondering where his friends might be.

As shadows stretched and giggles grew,
A hedgehog tried a limbo too.
The stars above were laughing loud,
As the night became a playful crowd.

Whispers of mischief filled the air,
With every twirl, each creature's flair.
Underneath the laughter's glow,
The tales of twilight start to flow.

Swaying Chants in the Flickering Light

The owl hooted a funky tune,
While mice tap-danced beneath the moon.
A raccoon played drums on a tin can,
All the critters joined in a wild jam plan.

The tall grass swayed with a charming wave,
As all animals prepared to rave.
A squirrel spun with nuts like a pro,
While a deer's spin made the laughter grow.

Giggling crickets sang off-beat,
While frogs formed a conga line on their feet.
An awkward turtle tried to groove,
As the stars gave him a playful move.

With hearts alight and spirits high,
They chanted songs to the whirling sky.
In the stillness, joy took flight,
In the flickering glow of the wild night.

Shimmering Mirage of the Night

Beneath the stars, a cat struck a pose,
Wearing a flower crown made of rose.
A fox held a mirror, checking his style,
Ensuring he danced with extra mile.

A wise old owl gave fashion advice,
Claiming that stripes could add some spice.
With every turn and hop and skip,
The night turned into a comical trip.

A porcupine donned a glittery cape,
Studying closely a mystical shape.
Twirling shadows made them all crack up,
As laughter overflowed in a joy-filled cup.

A raccoon filmed the scene with flair,
Catching every giggle in the air.
Making memories, they danced till late,
In the shimmering glow of fate.

Twilight's Kiss on Blooming Heartbeats

Twilight brushed against the blooms,
Chasing away their sleepy dooms.
With petals open wide and bright,
They giggled at the comical sight.

A bumblebee donned a tiny hat,
Buzzing jokes while chasing a mat.
He clumsily landed on a bloom,
Causing a flutter and a mini boom.

The daisies giggled, swayed in glee,
As insects joined their comedy spree.
A ladybug attempted a dance,
But tripped and fell, oh what a chance!

Hopping frogs sang silly rhymes,
Echoing through the moonlit climes.
In this magical floral bright,
Joy reigned over the playful night.

Starlit Reverie in the Glade

In the glade where critters dance,
A squirrel plots a silly chance.
He jumps with glee but lands with grace,
Right on a frog's surprised face!

Above, the stars twinkle and tease,
The raccoons giggle in the breeze.
They trade their masks for silly hats,
And practice their best acrobatics, like acrobatic bats.

A firefly bulbs with radiant glee,
Winking at a bumblebee.
They buzz around, creating a spark,
Hosting a party 'til after dark.

The owls hoot with laughing calls,
While moonbeams sneak and gently fall.
The night is young, the fun's in tow,
In the glade where the wild things glow!

A Serenade to the Night's Embrace

Under the sky's velvety shawl,
Bats play tag, while crickets call.
The dogs join in with howls of tune,
A raucous choir beneath the moon.

A hedgehog wobbles with flair and zest,
Challenging rabbits to a funny contest.
Each hops and tumbles in a jovial chase,
As laughter fills the leafy space.

The trees start shaking, swaying wild,
As squirrels pretend to be cloistered child.
Mocking the owls, with a hoot and cheer,
Conspiring mischief, never fear!

So gather round for a wild night,
With nature's pranks and pure delight.
In the embrace of gentle sway,
The silly shenanigans are here to stay!

Soft Glow Amidst the Wildflowers

Softly glowing near a patch of bloom,
The daisies giggle, banishing gloom.
A playful fox joins in the fun,
Dancing 'round, thinking he's won.

Butterflies flutter, pretentious prattlers,
While a snail spins tales of wintry battles.
The daisies crown him with petals bright,
Mimicking kings in the pale moonlight.

A ladybug tries to steal the show,
Proclaiming she's fast—oh, put on a show!
"Catch me if you can!" she giggles with flair,
As the flower-tots giggle and stare.

With soft whispers, the petals sway,
In a party of blooms till the break of day.
Softly glowing, mischief unplanned,
In the fields where tall grass stands!

Nocturnal Hues in the Open Air

Night paints the world with colors so bright,
As kangaroos hop in a comical flight.
They juggle shadows while leaping around,
Turning the field into a circus ground.

A chill raccoon struts with a hat so grand,
Holding a lantern in his small hand.
He winks at the stars and takes a bow,
Prompting a laugh from every "wow!"

The owls pretend to hold a debate,
"What's better: night or last week's plate?"
They hoot and holler over pizza crust,
Night is for laughter and friendships robust!

So let's bask in the hues of nighttime,
Where every joke is a spark in rhyme.
In the open air where silliness blends,
A magical night where the fun never ends!

The Universe Cradling the Earth

In the night, cows dance like stars,
They twirl and glide, oh, what bizarre!
Sheep wear hats and sing with glee,
While frogs debate on who's the best MC.

A rabbit hops with a moon-sized grin,
Telling tales of where the fun begins.
Owls wear glasses, reading the night,
Baffling bats with their jokes so bright.

Fireflies blink like disco balls,
Holding parties under the giant walls.
The grass giggles, tickled by the breeze,
As crickets tap dance, aiming to please.

Yet the universe chuckles, ever so sly,
As it watches the chaos with a twinkling eye.
Who knew at night, such fun would emerge,
With giggling critters, in a grand surge?

Mysteries of Darkness and Glimmering Skies

Bats in capes flit to and fro,
Superheroes of night, stealing the show.
Mice hold meetings with snacks in tow,
Discussing the latest cheese on the go.

Stars are giggling, a cosmic prank,
Throwing confetti from a shimmering tank.
The wind whispers jokes, oh what a delight,
As shadows do the cha-cha, into the night.

Squirrels in tuxedos act rather bold,
Trading secrets of nuts over tales retold.
The moon smirks, enjoying the jest,
As the night unfolds in a comical quest.

Wild adventures just waiting to hatch,
While owls hoot loudly, "Let's all make a catch!"
A mystery wrapped in starlight's embrace,
Where laughter erupts in the grand cosmic space.

Luna's Touch on the Gentle Landscape

At dusk, the daisies wear silly hats,
Joking with daisies and gossiping cats.
The trees tell tales of their ancient woes,
As night critters waltz on tiny toes.

The grass, a blanket for dreams to unfold,
Makes pillows for rabbits, stories retold.
While hedgehogs huddle, sharing their snacks,
Pondering deeply about the best tracks.

Frogs burst into song, a loud serenade,
While fireflies dance in a sparkling parade.
With each whispered chuckle, the night takes a turn,
For the joy of the dark is what we all yearn.

So raise a toast to the stars up high,
To the laughter and fun beneath the vast sky.
For even at night, the spirits are bright,
In a landscape adored, it's pure delight.

Night Hues Woven with Stardust

The night is a canvas, splashy and bright,
With colors of giggles that dance in delight.
A hedgehog prances with a flair so grand,
While flowers sway, making a rock band.

Caterpillars jive, in a club full of cheer,
Bouncing to rhythms, oh so clear.
Chipmunks debate the best cheese to eat,
Creating a feast that's quite the treat.

The wind carries laughter, a whimsical breeze,
As crickets orchestrate symphonies with ease.
Even the shadows, they shimmy along,
While night critters join in, singing their song.

So lie on the grass, let joy take the lead,
In the hues of the night, we sow laughter's seed.
For in this tapestry woven so gleefully,
The magic of night brings pure jubilee.

Luminescence Where the Wild Things Roam

In the field, creatures prance,
Under bright beams, they dance.
A cow wears shades, so cool,
While chickens play hopscotch, like fools.

A pig in a tutu twirls with flair,
Bouncing off grass, without a care.
The sheep hold a disco ball high,
As fireflies buzz like a DJ nearby.

A goat sips tea, loudly slurping,
Says, "These hooves are always burping!"
The moon cracks jokes, funny and slick,
As critters laugh, they can't help but tick.

In this glow, with leaps and glows,
Every silly idea surely flows.
With wild things strutting in the night,
It's a festive madness, pure delight!

Midnight's Brush on Nature's Palette

Nature's colors go wacky tonight,
With squirrels donning hats, what a sight!
The canvas glows, and then it winks,
As frogs in tuxedos tap dance, with clinks.

A rabbit paints stars with its paw,
While owls hoot jokes that leave us in awe.
The night sky giggles at the scene,
And grasshoppers hop like they're on caffeine.

With shimmering leaves that shimmer and swirl,
The dandelions twirl, giving each a whirl.
Bumblebees toast with nectar so sweet,
While critters gather 'round for a midnight treat.

In this bright chaotic show,
Where laughter and colors boldly flow,
The brush of night has its playful side,
As every beast lets their giggles glide.

Glowing Spirits Beneath the Timid Sky

Beneath the stars, the air's so light,
A cat plans pranks with all its might.
Glowworms giggle in mushroom hats,
While raccoons play poker with sassy chats.

A turtle rides a skateboard, what a thrill,
While ants have a race down a tiny hill.
The wind whispers jokes to the trees,
And even the daisies are chuckling with ease.

Fireflies flash their glow like lights,
Trying to win over the bug's delights.
A ladybug juggles and nearly slips,
The tiniest of giggles escape from their lips.

With spirits bright, they dance and sway,
In this merry night, hip-hip-hooray!
What a sight, creatures so spry,
In a world that shimmers, they all fly high.

Dance of Light Among the Tall Grasses

In tall grass, the sparkles prance,
While crickets do a silly dance.
A hedgehog rolls, all puffed and round,
As the night giggles at the sound.

Fireflies sway, like they know the tune,
While bunnies jump like they're on a balloon.
The stars peek down with a twinkling eye,
Join this dance, oh me, oh my!

A squirrel squirrels away a birthday cake,
As raccoons clap, for goodness' sake!
The moon struts in a sparkling cape,
Making shadows that twist and gape.

As laughter resonates through the night,
Every critter feels the delight.
So, come take part in this festive cheer,
In the glow where mischief draws near!

Shadows Swaying under Cosmic Sight

In the field, shadows dance around,
Crickets chirp with a funny sound.
A rabbit hops, thinking it's grand,
While a turtle claims he's in a band.

Fireflies waltz like they're on a spree,
Whispering secrets to the tall grass knee.
The owl hoots with a clever wit,
While the fox smirks, thinking he's it.

Starlight and Secrets Between the Grass

Stars twinkle like they're playing tag,
The night air filled with a playful brag.
A mouse shares jokes with a cheeky squirrel,
While a deer rolls its eyes in a whirl.

The breeze giggles, teasing the leaves,
As crickets form a band with their sleeves.
A hedgehog slips, does a little flip,
While the night laughs, giving him a tip.

Nurtured by the Softness of Night

The grass tickles feet in the dark,
A hedgehog sings to his night-time park.
Fireflies blink like stars gone rogue,
As a raccoon pranks in his own little vogue.

The sky wears a velvet, cheeky grin,
While the tulips sway, inviting a spin.
Bunnies tumble, thinking it's grand,
With laughter echoing across the land.

Echoes of Serenity and Light

Under the stars, the laughter flows,
A sleepy owl yawns, hiding his toes.
A raccoon dives into a pie,
While the fireflies giggle, oh my oh my!

The shadows chuckle behind every tree,
As nighttime creatures join in with glee.
The moon winks down, in the sky so bright,
As all gather 'round for a fun-filled night.

Celestial Secrets in the Night Air

Under the sky, the critters prance,
Bugs doing the tango, a funny dance.
Owls roll their eyes, as if to say,
"Why do they party? It's night, not day!"

Grasshoppers chirp, with a laugh, quite spry,
While fireflies flash like they're saying hi.
A raccoon with a hat flips pancakes at dawn,
"What a night!" he exclaims, as the moon fades on.

Radiant Threads on a Woven Night

A spider spins tales in the silvery dew,
"Have you heard the one about the kangaroo?"
Crickets provide the punchline with glee,
"Hop on over!" they chirp, "Join our spree!"

The stars are all laughing, in twinkling delight,
As hedgehogs juggle, quite the funny sight.
A cow jumps a fence, tries to leap into air,
Lands in a patch of flowers—a splendid affair.

Dappled Illumination in Twilight's Shroud

A porcupine sneezes, it goes with a flair,
Scaring the skunks who were just standing there.
They zip to the shadows, saying, "What was that?"
Only to find out, it was just a cat.

The moonbeams giggle, shining down bright,
While a badger plays chess with a squirrel that night.
"Checkmate!" cries the badger, with utmost pride,
Squirrel throws acorns and runs off to hide.

Serenade of Stars Over the Meadow's Edge

In the still of the night, the laughter does soar,
As a turkey sings opera, oh what a roar!
The stars join in, with a glittery cheer,
"Encore!" yells a fox, with a loud, booming jeer!

A raccoon on drums, giving it all he's got,
As the frogs croak along, right on the spot.
The night blooms with giggles, under shimmering skies,
While everyone knows, it's the best of times!

Dancing Shadows on Dewy Grasses

In the dark, the critters prance,
With wobbly legs, they take a chance.
A rabbit hops, a frog does leap,
And all around, the giggles seep.

The fireflies blink, their dance a show,
While ants march in a goofy row.
A mouse with a hat, oh what a sight!
He twirls around, outshining the night.

Dewy blades glisten, a slippery floor,
As everyone slips and falls to the floor.
Who knew a waltz could cause such a fuss?
In the grass, they roll, all covered in dust.

With laughter echoing through the trees,
The night is filled with mischief and tease.
They dance till dawn, all tired and silly,
Under the stars, feeling light and frilly.

Night's Serenade Beneath the Stars

The crickets sing a tune so bright,
While possums waltz under starlight.
A raccoon with a crown takes the lead,
Galloping about with utmost speed.

The owls hoot, keep time with the beat,
As frogs jump in, with rhythm neat.
Each animal joins in, a grand parade,
Making the night a wild escapade.

With twinkling lights and shadows that sway,
The creatures laugh and dance away.
A hedgehog spins, all prickly and round,
Creating a spectacle, silliness abound.

In this chorus of giggles, the fun won't cease,
As the night wraps up in playful peace.
With tired limbs and dreams in sight,
They drift to sleep, content in their delight.

Luminous Dreams on a Velvet Night

A kitten yawns under silvery beams,
Chasing at shadows, lost in dreams.
A playful breeze whispers sweetly in,
As small feet prance, and chuckles begin.

The twinkling stars seem to wink and tease,
While a dog dances, as happy as you please.
A butterfly flutters, too bold to confess,
Landing on noses, causing a mess.

With giggles raining, the night feels bright,
As everyone juggles with all of their might.
A squirrel drops acorns, a clumsy feat,
Surely a sign that the night's a treat!

As laughter crescendos and the fun rolls on,
The velvet sky signals that soon it's dawn.
Through silly antics and joyous prance,
The night turns to memory in laughter's dance.

The Glow of Night's Embrace

In the dusk, the glow brings delight,
A dancing mouse calls it a night!
With each tiny step and charming twirl,
He spins round fast, such a silly whirl.

The owls debate who's the best singer,
While the raccoons munch, sneaking a linger.
A bat flaps by, shouting, "Look at me!"
As the stars above giggle with glee.

With hiccuping frogs joining the fun,
Their musical antics have just begun.
They croak out ballads, offbeat and wide,
As fireflies skip, lighting up their pride.

In this glow, the silliness flows,
With laughter and mischief, the night surely glows.
As dawn yawns softly, the fun still thrives,
In dreams of the night, the joy survives.

Whispers Beneath the Starlit Rays

In the night, a rabbit pranced,
Wearing socks and doing a dance.
His fluffy tail a little too bright,
Claiming he's king of the night!

The hedgehogs chuckled, rolling on by,
As the raccoon's tied a bowtie.
They argued over who wore it best,
While the crickets waved, all impressed.

A lost owl gave a hoot, quite loud,
Startled a cow who mooed out proud.
"I swear I saw a ghost tonight!"
"Just a shadow," squeaked the tiny sprite.

Beneath the glow, mischief was clear,
Every creature filled with cheer.
So let's dance till the break of day,
When it's time for silly games to play!

The Embrace of the Gentle Night

A cheeky squirrel climbed a tree,
To catch a breeze and sip iced tea.
He spilled it all on a sleepy hare,
Who jumped high, with a startled stare!

The fireflies flickered, looking confused,
As a tiny mouse danced, feeling bruised.
He tripped over a twig, fell with a thud,
Splashed in the puddle, made such a flood!

The wise old owl criticized the ruck,
"Can't you guys try to avoid such luck?"
But the others just giggled and rolled with glee,
Saying, "Life's more fun with a splash of spree!"

As the stars winked with laughter and cheer,
A night of mischief was finally here.
So gather your friends, let joy ignite,
In a world where whimsy takes flight!

Shimmering Echoes in Midnight Hues

Beneath the twinkle, a frog sang loud,
With a top hat, looking like quite the crowd.
The turtles grooved, so smooth and spry,
In a conga line that caught the eye!

A curious bat did a little flip,
While a turtle tried to join the trip.
"Don't rush, my friends," he called with glee,
"We'll reach the end, eventually!"

The raccoon chef cooked blueberry pie,
But then got sticky, oh my, oh my!
The snacks went flying, a food fight ensued,
"Let's eat instead!" shouted the raccoon dude.

In the night hues, laughter echoed bright,
With stars above to guide their sight.
So when the fun's got you feeling bold,
Just remember: tales shared are better than gold!

Dance of the Fireflies in the Dark

In the dark, where the fireflies twirl,
A pig in a tutu began to swirl.
With a snort and a squeal, he led the show,
While the owl hooted, putting on a glow!

A goofy raccoon wore mismatched socks,
While chasing after some sneaky rocks.
He tripped and tumbled, rolling away,
And laughed at himself, it made his day!

The night was alive, filled with fun and cheer,
As chipmunks gathered with cookies near.
They tossed them high, flew like kites,
Giggling at their delightful sights.

So come join the dance, let joy collide,
With wobbly moves and hearts open wide.
Under the stars where silliness sparks,
Celebrate life till the morning larks!

The Ethereal Call of the Night

In the dark, the critters dance,
Chasing shadows, taking a chance.
A raccoon plays hide and seek,
While frogs croak tunes, oh so unique.

Stars above giggle and spark,
Beneath them, owls hoot in the dark.
A squirrel slips, then takes a bow,
Waving proudly, look at me now!

Fireflies flicker, a light parade,
Over the grass, a luminous braid.
A chubby rabbit munches a snack,
With crumbs on his chin, he looks so whack!

This serene night, with laughter we share,
The forest floor becomes our fair.
Nature's jesters, what a sight,
Under the glow of the cozy night!

Illuminated Pathways Through the Quiet

Jesters of the night prance 'round,
Making merry with every sound.
A hedgehog rolls, a comical spree,
As if the grass tickles his knee.

Tall blades sway, like they're in on a joke,
The moonlit air, a puff of smoke.
A wandering sheep tries to sing,
But it sounds more like a rubber band's twang!

Glowing orbs buzz without a care,
While the bored badger leans on the lamb's hair.
They giggle at clouds that drift and bloat,
"A marshmallow just fell from a goat!"

Beneath the sparkle, laughter ignites,
In this bizarre world of delightful sights.
With each chuckle, the night grows bright,
As critters bask in the gentle light.

Night Blossoms in Soft Radiance

Whiskers twitch in the soft glow,
A dance of shadows as they flow.
A cat struts, thinking she's a queen,
While a mouse just gasps, "Oh, what's that sheen?"

A hedgehog sneezes—what a sight!
Scattering leaves in pure delight.
Then a goofy goat joins the spree,
With a twirling leap, "Look at me!"

Flowers giggle, swaying in time,
To the rhythm of crickets' chime.
Each petal whispers a little tease,
"Why do you skip? Just move with ease!"

As stars twinkle and chortle on high,
The night unfolds a silly sigh.
Here in the glow, all worries flee,
While laughter weaves through each tree!

Glowing Embrace of the Silent Night

In the hush of night, a party begins,
With chipmunks outdoing their spins.
A bugle beetle plays a tune,
While a skunk dances beneath the moon!

Dandelions giggle, seeds in flight,
Carried away like balloons from a sight.
A timid deer joins, all playful and coy,
While the fireflies cheer, filled with joy.

Tickles of grass, soft and spry,
Bouncing around like they can fly.
The barn owl chuckles with delight,
At the rabbit's somersaults tonight!

In the gentle spark of the evening's weave,
The laughter sings, and we believe.
Under this blanket of peculiar hue,
Funny moments come to view!

Visions of Tranquility and Soft Light

Beneath a bulbous glow, we prance,
The bunnies dance, a funny chance.
They wear their hats and twirl around,
While crickets play a silly sound.

The fireflies flicker, joke and jest,
With lanterns on their tiny chests.
A squirrel in shades zips by with glee,
For nighttime parties, he must be free.

A deer, bemused, joins in the game,
Her awkward moves—Oh, what a shame!
But laughter ripples through the glade,
In cozy corners, dreams are laid.

So here's to nights of frolic, cheer,
Where even shadows chortle near.
In nature's humor, we delight,
As stars above twinkle with spite.

Reflections of Heaven on Earthly Tides

The moon's a pie, that glows with pride,
Hungry frogs sit side by side.
They croak their tune, a chorus loud,
Enticing bugs to join the crowd.

A turtle slips, a little too slick,
Chasing shadows, what a trick!
He thinks he's fast, but watch him glide,
As he naps and flips, quite dignified.

The crickets challenge, one by one,
Who can chirp the wittiest pun?
They have their battles, short and sweet,
Each taking turns, a sound retreat.

Yet nature laughs, its jesters bold,
In this dark show, where fun unfolds.
With every quirk, we see them shine,
Sharing stories under the divine.

Night Melodies Through Blooming Meadows

The flowers giggle, petals bright,
Swaying gently in the night.
Their whispers dance on breezes light,
While raccoons throw a stealthy fight.

A hedgehog dons a sparkly crown,
As owls hoot softly, wearing frowns.
They ponder life and sip their tea,
While shadows sway in jubilee.

The daisies tease the sleepy grass,
"Come join us, friend! Don't be a sass!"
The blades all chuckle, weave a tale,
Of every critter brave and pale.

And as the stars wink in delight,
This meadow party lasts till light.
In laughter's echo, wild and free,
We find our joy in this decree.

Enchanted Evenings of Soft Glimmers

Under glowing orbs we waddle and weave,
While cheeky mice plot to deceive.
They plot a prank with shiny things,
And giggles dance where laughter rings.

The owl takes bets on the night's plan,
Who'll steal the cheese? That's the scam!
With whiskers twitching, they all conspire,
To lift the spoils, they feel the fire.

A hedgehog slips in pursuit of fame,
But trips on roots, oh what a game!
The moon's a witness to this wild spree,
With each little mishap, we all agree.

In this enchanted space of mirth,
Where chuckles echo, joy gives birth.
What tales we weave in glowing beams,
With every twinkle, life is dreams.

Dreamweaver's Dance in the Night

In shadows deep, the critters prance,
They have a wiggle and a silly dance.
A grasshopper tried to steal the show,
But tripped and fell, oh what a blow!

The fireflies flicker like tiny stars,
They swoop and dive, like wild guitars.
The toads croak loudly, think they are grand,
While the mice plot mischief, a fun little band!

A whimsical breeze gives the trees a swish,
The owls hoot high, adding to the wish.
A fox with a hat struts with flair,
As rabbits giggle without a care!

So let's join the folly beneath the sky,
With laughter and joy, we twirl and fly.
In this dreamweaver's realm, so bright and bold,
Where wittiness reigns and stories unfold!

Celestial Glow on Nature's Canvas

A squirrel juggles acorns, chasing a cat,
While the owls just snicker, sitting quite flat.
The daisies are winking, they giggle in green,
As the daisies tell jokes, the funniest seen.

Beneath a sprinkle of stardust and cheer,
The critters roast marshmallows, sipping on beer.
The badgers wear hats; they think they're quite sly,
While hedgehogs giggle with a gleam in their eye.

A raccoon with shades glances over his stash,
While the fireflies twirl in a grand little flash.
And the wind gives a chuckle, a tickle to trees,
As we dance with the bugs, playful as bees!

An evening adorned in delight and fun,
Where the humor is bright, and laughter has won.
In this canvas of life, under shimmering lights,
The giggles of nature take fantastic flights!

Illuminated Silence of the Grove

In the grove where the crickets perform a tune,
A raccoon is slip-sliding beneath the moon.
He trips on a root, with a flail and a flip,
While fireflies watch with a chuckle and quip.

The owls make wisecracks from high on their perch,
While young foxes, all bundled, in laughter they lurch.
A turtle in shades, oh so cool and so sly,
Sips from a puddle, just passing on by.

Mice in their jackets prepare for the show,
With acorn confetti all set on the low.
They dance in a circle, a skipping ballet,
While squirrels practice their nutty cabaret!

With a teasing breeze casting whispers around,
They gather for giggles, where laughter is found.
In the silence adorned, funny moments ignite,
As the grove comes alive in this whimsical night!

Ethereal Radiance Over the Plains

On the vast plains where the starglow beams,
The creatures assemble, chasing their dreams.
A cow with a bowtie starts mooing a beat,
While goats wear sombreros that can't be beat!

A chicken in glasses holds court with the sheep,
As they giggle at jokes that will make you weep.
The cacti grow taller to catch every jest,
While the owls hoot softly, they're quite unimpressed.

The bunnies are breakdancing under the sky,
While the cows do the cha-cha, oh my, oh my!
A crow's wearing sneakers, strutting around,
With laughter and echo, the night's savoring sound.

So join in the frolic, beneath the night's charm,
In a world of delight where there's no need for alarm.
Under celestial gleam, where humor remains,
Riding the wave of those joy-filled plains!

The Glow of Ancestral Night

Under the stars, the cows conspire,
Swapping tall tales of how they admire.
Spooky stories of ghosts and fright,
While munching on grass in the soft, cool night.

The crickets join in with a chirpy song,
Annoying the owls who think they're too strong.
A dance-off begins under twinkling lights,
As frogs jump in with their wobbly sights.

Beneath the old oak, a raccoon jives,
Telling the ghost that it barely survives.
They share a good laugh, leave the fright behind,
In this magical realm, joy's easy to find.

The moon's just a bulb, for the party planned,
As fireflies buzz around, joining the band.
The night's really wild, with secrets to share,
In the glow of the dark, it's beyond compare.

Enchanted Shadows and Gentle Breezes

In the cool dusk, the shadows play,
As squirrels throw nuts like grenades in the fray.
A hedgehog rolls by, thinking it's sly,
While the turtles slow dance, making sparks fly.

The grass whispers secrets, the daisies all giggle,
As a clumsy deer attempts to just wiggle.
A firefly zips past, thinking it's grand,
While field mice form bands, playing in sand.

Laughter erupts as the rabbits all race,
Chasing their tails, it's a silly embrace.
The stars are all watching, they can't help but grin,
At the hilarity wrapped in the nighttime skin.

The breeze carries whispers of chuckles and cheers,
From owls giving advice based on their years.
In this joyful frolic, where laughter takes flight,
Every creature joins in, lighting up the night.

Silent Conversations in the Dark

Beneath the vast sky, the critters all chat,
About who's the best at finding a hat.
The bunnies debate, with their ears all a-flop,
While a wise old fox just can't take a stop.

A squirrel gets tangled in vines as it talks,
Demanding a truce from the keen-eyed hawks.
The owls blink down, with a humorous glare,
Listening in on this hilarious affair.

Grasshoppers clank, with their dancing and leaps,
While a sleepy badger just dreams and peeps.
What a peculiar sight, in the dense, cool night,
As laughter erupts, making shadows take flight.

A moonbeam slips in, making faces so bright,
While everyone giggles at this cheerful sight.
In the quiet of dark, where jests freely spark,
The fun is contagious, igniting a lark.

Light of the Hidden Glade

In a glade far away, the creatures convene,
With secrets and snacks, and giggles unseen.
The bumblebees buzz like a marching parade,
As the dancing ferns sway in the cool evening shade.

A quick-footed deer plays tag with a hare,
While a sneaky raccoon sneaks snacks from the air.
The owl joins the fray, flapping wings all about,
Clumsily tumbling, it's just one big shout.

The whispers all mingle with laughter and glee,
As hedgehogs roll 'round, full of mischief and spree.
The stars all twinkle, loving quirks of the night,
As the glow from the glade sets everything light.

So here in the woods, under laughter's soft flare,
Where each silly mishap is treated with care.
In this joyful retreat, where friendships ignite,
The hidden glade sparkles with pure delight.

Celestial Reflections on the Earth

Bright stars wink at me, oh what a sight,
Grass tickles my toes, a sheer delight.
Dancing fireflies join the silly parade,
I trip on a rock, oh the fun we made!

Whispers of crickets sing a strange tune,
A raccoon's nose peeks out, too curious too soon.
I share my secrets, hoping he'll share,
He snickers and scurries, I swear he doesn't care!

The sky stretches wide, a canvas so vast,
I challenge the clouds, let's see who's the fastest!
They puff up in laughter, drifting with glee,
While I chase their shadows, a sight to see!

In the night's embrace, my laughter resounds,
Nature's my audience, joyfulness abounds.
As the world spins softly, I can't help but grin,
This wild night of whimsy, let the fun begin!

A Nighttalk with the Stillness

Under the whispering trees, I sit and plot,
Why does the silence feel like a lot?
The owls keep hooting, asking me to chat,
I tell them my secrets, they just blink and flap!

Asteroids zoom by, racing away,
I challenge a comet, let's play a game today!
But it laughs and zooms off, far out of reach,
While I ponder my victory, what can I teach?

The breeze plays tag, tickling my ears,
But watch out for cobwebs, they'll catch all my cheers!
In the still of the night, laughter is found,
As a chorus of creatures join in, all around.

With shadows as partners, in this dance of delight,
I waltz with my worries, beneath stars so bright.
If only the stillness could crack a good joke,
We'd laugh 'til the dawn, until it awoke!

Ethereal Beams and Hidden Paths

Glowing trails beckon, where should I go?
A toad hops by, laughing at my slow flow.
I try to keep up, but he hops with such flair,
I trip on my shoelace—oh, a night to declare!

The wind carries tidbits of stories untold,
While shadows dance merrily, daring the bold.
A butterfly giggles, all dressed up in stripes,
"Catch me if you can!"—what a night full of gripes!

A gopher pops up, just to lend me a hand,
"Follow my burrow—you'll find ice cream stand!"
But wait, is that fantasy? I tread with some care,
Into the unknown, where laughter fills the air!

Lost in the magic, under skies filled with cheer,
Each hidden path whispers, "Adventure is near!"
A giggle from a hedgehog seals the pact tight,
This night, filled with giggles, is pure delight!

Twinkling Secrets Among the Wildflowers

Beneath the glimmers, wildflowers sway,
I share my stories, they nod in dismay.
"Did you hear that?" the daisies combine,
As I spin tales of mischief and wine!

A tomato plant argues, "I'm quite round and ripe!"
While I chuckle at peas, forming a type.
"Let's start a band!" yells a bold, sprightly fern,
And the tulips shift, waiting for their turn!

With blossoms as buddies, we sway and we sway,
Giggling softly as night turns to day.
The moon dangles low, catching earfuls of fun,
A blooming friendship, beneath each star run.

As insects join in, a parade of delights,
With the sway of the petals, we forget our plights.
In this floral concert, laughter's our cue,
Under the twinkling mysteries, we bloom, too!

Lush Lullabies Under Celestial Skin

Bunnies hop with shoes too big,
They sing their tunes, a cheeky jig.
The grass is soft, the stars they wink,
While cows all gather for a drink.

A fox in shades does strut around,
Holding court, quite proud, quite sound.
While owls hoot jokes that make us grin,
And we all join in, let's spin, let's spin!

The crickets chirp a catchy beat,
With fireflies dancing on tiny feet.
A rabbit jokes, 'I lost my hat!'
And all the critters all go, 'How fat!'

So under skies of twinkling lights,
We laugh and play through silly nights.
Elders chuckle, kids just tease,
In dreams, we all become the breeze.

Flickering Lanterns of the Night

Fireflies flicker, like tiny lamps,
They dance around, doing funny pramps.
A snail races slow, but claims he's fast,
While frogs critique his hopping cast.

The owls wear glasses, examining sights,
As raccoons plan their late-night flights.
Sparrows argue over snacks to share,
While sleepy kittens just stare with flair.

A hedgehog pricks the air with a joke,
Says, 'I'm not sharp, just give me a poke!'
The night crew giggles, can't hold it in,
As stars scatter coins, let the fun begin!

Whiskers twitch, a mouse tickles a bat,
Together they giggle, just imagine that!
In this vast garden, wit takes flight,
As laughter echoes through the gentle night.

Silvery Threads in the Quiet Pasture

Mice in vests hold dance-offs bold,
While sheep spin tales that never get old.
A goat plays guitar, quite out of tune,
But everyone sways, bouncing to the moon.

A chicken sports a shimmering crown,
Says, 'Cluck it up!', never wears a frown.
The owls hoot softly, 'What's the ruckus?',
'Time for a laugh and some good old luck us!'

While daisies gossip, their petals aflutter,
A curious cow shouts, 'What's the matter?'
'It's just a party!' the fireflies beam,
Leading the charge, like a vibrant dream.

So come and join us, the night is young,
With laughter and chatter, we're all so sprung.
In fields where silliness takes a dare,
We'll weave the night, with joy to spare.

Conversations with the Night Breeze

The wind whispers secrets, a breeze in the trees,
A squirrel chomps loudly on acorns with ease.
It shouts, 'Hey, look!', as shadows in play,
Twist and dance while the night hides away.

A raccoon shares tales, funny and bright,
Of sneaky escapades under the light.
While turtles debate who's winning this sprint,
Though all they're doing is blinking and squint.

The stars join the fun, twinkling with glee,
As frogs croak a beat in a new symphony.
A cow jokes about how she learned to moo,
'With all this laughter, I'll never feel blue!'

Secret chats with the night breeze carry,
Who's bringing the snacks? Oh! That's quite merry.
So gather around as we sip the cool air,
And share in the fun, without a care.

The Glimmering Meadow's Secret

The crickets hold a conference,
Deciding if the grass should dance.
A hedgehog makes a clumsy move,
The flowers giggle, lost in trance.

Beneath a sky so shiny bright,
A rabbit tries to steal a snack.
He thinks he's sneaky, oh what a sight!
But ends up with a pie on his back.

A deer winks at the owl on high,
"This party's wild! Let's eat a cake!"
The owl just blinks, starts to sigh,
That deer, so bold, oh what a mistake!

While shadows play in cheeky ways,
The stars like toys in frolic spin.
The meadow giggles through the haze,
Where laughter reigns, and dreams begin.

Enchanted Nightfall Over the Pasture

When twilight wraps the world in glee,
A cow attempts a ballet twist.
But tripped by grass, she lets out a plea,
"Oh dear, must I exist like this?"

The fireflies play hopscotch in air,
With lightning bugs cheering from the side.
The jokes they tell, so light and rare,
Make even the moonbeam chuckle and glide.

A goat wears shades, likes to pose,
Pretending he's the king of style.
But tripping over fallen rose,
He joins the laughter for a while.

In playful tones and antics bright,
The night unfolds its silly schemes.
As creatures chirp with sheer delight,
The pasture dances in our dreams.

Moonlit Reveries Beneath Ancient Boughs

Beneath the trees, a raccoon pranks,
Sneaking snacks from a picnic spread.
He giggles deep, his sides he ranks,
As squirrels shout, "Who's the breadhead?"

An owl offers a stand-up set,
With jokes about the cattle's flair.
Though puns are weak, the crowd's all wet,
The laughter flows like woodland air.

A hedgehog dons a tiny hat,
Declaring a dance-off in the glen.
But instead of moves, he rather sat,
And rolled away from would-be fans.

While shadows creep and stories spin,
The night laughs hard in silly ways.
Nature's jesters play to win,
As dreams take flight in moonlit rays.

A Symphony of Glow and Whisper

The nighttime features a quirky band,
A frog on drums, a mouse on keys.
They break the rules, so out of hand,
The fireflies dance, laughing with ease.

A cow's offbeat, the sheep try too,
A chorus of bleats that's far from right.
While crickets join in the hullabaloo,
They rock the night with pure delight.

The grass tickles ankles, laughter spreads,
As owls keep time with their wise old hoots.
The moon cracks jokes in my tangled head,
While trees sway softly in silly suits.

And as the stars join in the spree,
An echo of joy fills the air.
Tonight is wild, let spirits be,
Where every creature has room to share.

Radiant Paths Through Silent Domains

A dance of shadows on the grass,
The crickets chirp, oh what a class!
The fireflies buzz like they're in charge,
While rabbits hop, and squirrels enlarge.

With every step, a giggle grows,
As hedgehogs poke their nighttime toes.
A raccoon sings some off-key song,
While owls laugh, 'Can't we all get along?'

The grasshoppers leap with style and flair,
One trips, then tumbles—oh, what a scare!
The moon peeks through, a celestial spy,
Just waiting for the next big fly-by.

In this wild realm, the creatures cheer,
"Let's celebrate, for we've no fear!"
As the stars twinkle, the night gets bright,
In radiant paths, all feels just right.

Luminescent Hues of the Twilight Tides

The sky spills colors, orange and blue,
While ants perform a conga, just for you!
The sleepy sheep doze, dreams a-fluff,
As they plot to conquer this night-time stuff.

Bunnies don hats, thinking they're quite slick,
They hop and laugh, oh what a trick!
The glow of night makes all things bold,
As possums strut, acting quite old.

A raccoon steers a tiny boat,
While crabs take selfies, keen as a goat.
Fireflies blink like little stars,
Dancing 'round in a game of guitars.

The fun's not done; let's raise a cheer,
For the glow of the night brings us near.
In hues of twilight, all creatures play,
Making mischief 'til the break of day.

Nocturnal Echoes in the Open Meadow

The frogs croak out a cheesy rhyme,
While owls plot mischief, oh so sublime.
A fox in a top hat struts with pride,
As squirrels giggle and the raccoons hide.

Bouncing about, a field mouse twirls,
With tiny tap shoes, he gives it a whirl.
Behind the thistles, shadows prance,
Collecting laughter, they join the dance.

As the cool breeze brings some sweet delight,
A lizard claims to be the king of the night.
His crown is made of twigs and leaves,
The audience laughs, and the night believes.

With echoes ringing through the dark,
The meadow's a stage, a flamboyant park.
As critters guffaw, we all agree,
This nocturnal realm is wild and free!

Starlit Chants and Flickering Hues

In the realm where shadows tease,
Critters chirp with utmost ease.
A hedgehog shimmies and shakes his spine,
While fireflies dance, oh how they shine.

Chanting echoes filled with whim,
As the night grows plump and dim.
A chipmunk tries to show some flair,
But tumbles over without a care.

The stars above seem to burst with laughter,
As squirrels race, each chasing after.
With giggling glee, the night comes alive,
As every creature gives it a jive.

So let's all sing, our voices blend,
In this weird night, where laughter won't end.
Through flickering hues, we find our fun,
Under the watch of the sleeping sun.

www.ingramcontent.com/pod-product-compliance
Lightning Source LLC
Chambersburg PA
CBHW071818160426
43209CB00003B/129